Contents

Foreword

Revolutionaries, Visionaries, Creatives, Small Business Owners, Rejects and Casualties! People who have struggled for a cause, an idea, the self and the future. These people I speak of all have a reason to create and share and have for centuries. In the previous Century, these people have been largely excluded from the big studios and legacy media. Account Executives at Radio and TV Stations saw them as unhinged, damaging to profit margins, and offensive to the public. One can only imagine their shock when the Interactive Advertising Bureau (IAB) and PricewaterhouseCoopers (PwC) projected the podcast industry to be worth $4 billion.

The new age of media, ushered in by decentralized platforms such as YouTube, X, Spotify, various RSS Feeds and Websites are responsible for the vast changes in our society. Public discourse, access to information, growth of small businesses and greater accessibility to create have all been possible to the aforementioned platforms embracing the Libertarian nature of the early internet and especially the pirate radio movement and groundbreaking whistleblowers of the mid to late 20th Century. Without these pioneers of liberty, expression and American grit, we would not have been able to see the true effect of our current decentralized media landscape.

Podcasting is one of the major ways the average person can speak their mind and showcase topics and people they themselves feel important, not corporate bureaucrats. Podcasting is not only a great tool for expression; it is also a great tool for service based small businesses to create advertising content, giving them an edge they previously never had with traditional print advertising. This has allowed thousands of small, service-based businesses to open themselves to new clientele that can provide a decent life for themselves and their families. Podcasting is not the only tool at the people's disposal to be heard, marketable, and creative.

Social Media, the leading cause of degeneracy to some, a beacon of hope for the small business or creative, and the best way to shut the brain off for most. Social Media has changed society and is here to stay whether most like it or not. This topic will be difficult, complex, and exciting to explore, and I am personally excited to share with all of you the intricacies this tool has presented to us. I am excited to share the hopes many of my clients have, finally being able to access thousands if not millions of their target demographic for a fraction of what traditional media cost in the last century. I am also excited to tackle the common criticisms of the tool, most of which I agree with, and some I disagree with. Such a tool, elusive and a headache to many, has required experts to use and teach the tool to the masses.

The Modern Media Company rises to such an occasion. Sleek, savvy and oftentimes manned by staff no older than 30, has been the saving grace or the bane of existence for small business owners. This book aims to give the reader a basic understanding of media history; the ethical background media companies should have in guiding their direction and an unbiased look at the benefits and harms caused by advancing communications technology.

-Anthony Giorgio Barone, President of Barone Media Solutions, INC.

Piracy to

Podcasts

It is a cold November day. The year is 1920 and you are sitting with your family in your tight kitchen. You have just finished dinner, but the excitement of hearing the wireless crackle to life seemed to take your appetite away. This would be the first time Americans could listen to the results of a Presidential Election in their own homes. As the clock struck 6'o clock, you turned the dial and heard the wireless roar to life with its crackle and dull hum. You hear Leo Rosenberg, the Host for the evening, read out the following, "This is 8ZZ of the Westinghouse Electric and Manufacturing Company in East Pittsburgh, Pennsylvania."

(Leo Rosenberg broadcasting the Harding-Cox presidential election returns. Pictured are R.S. McClelland, William Thomas, Rosenberg, and John Frazier. From https://pittsburghantiqueradiosociety.org)

With the sparks that powered that first commercial broadcast in 1920, a raging fire has spread across the nation that has been burning endlessly for over 100 years. Radio in the United States did not just randomly appear overnight. The first known radio communications were reported in 1890. At that point it was mostly reserved for the United States Navy and amateurs who were able to get ahold of the equipment. Radio and its popularity became almost non-existent when the United States entered World War I.

On April 6, 1917, President Woodrow Wilson ordered the Federal Government to shutdown most civilian radio stations. This was done with the intent to prevent espionage and to cease any propaganda the Central Powers may have been spreading through the airwaves. Sadly, this censorship laid out the groundwork for further encroachments and regulations following the lifting of the radio ban when World War I officially ended in 1919 with the treaty of Versailles.

With the mind blowing potential for radio to unite, disseminate, criticize and propagandize came the governments fearful eye and heavy-handed regulations that have persisted as technology has evolved. The free, open form and unregulated medium that was radio is currently found with the vast lawlessness of the internet close to 100 years later. This heavy-handed regulation of radio, coupled with the overarching theme of repression that can be found in the first and second Red Scare.

The Second Red Scare saw the purging of Hollywood, Academia, Unions and the Political

Landscape in Washington. Anyone that was not decidedly pro-NATO, pro war and pro big business was unfairly labeled as a communist, lost their jobs, marriages, friends, and even their lives. These crackdowns on the American communist movement fractured the political landscape, leading to the very odd politics of the left today. The Communist Party was banned, creating a "vacuum" that needed to be filled by those that held socialist, unionist, and communist views with no organized party to lead the way. This paved the way for the "New Left" that emerged in the 1960's and 1970's.

The New Left gave birth to a new way of thinking. The Old Left of the Communist Party believed that class conflict, the wealthy exploiting the poor, was the disease cause of all suffering, symptoms of this disease manifested as social ills like racism and would only be resolved through political revolution through the ballot box or the cartridge box. The New Left believed that the main driver of oppression and suffering was racism, sexism, homophobia, symptoms that were not connected to a disease but rather considered diseases in themselves. Organizations of the New Left, like La Raza Unida, Student Nonviolent Coordinating Committee (SNCC) and many others needed a way to share this new way of thinking, as well as their anti-war stances at the onset of the Vietnam War.

This led to an explosion of underground newspapers, music, magazines, cinema, and pirate radio stations. Rock and Roll was a way to express this new way of viewing the world and destroying the old. The aim of this new genre was the "erasing [of] false categories of art, class, race, privatism, and the gap between audience and performer." [1](Morgan, *Retreating Inward* 1991). This attitude perfectly encapsulates the aims of the New Left, which has its roots in the modern progressive movement of today, to eliminate everything in the organized and structured world and to revert to our primal form of societal organization. While this book does not aim to go into the weeds of political movements, or my opinion of them, it is important to analyze the New Left as it is directly responsible for birthing the

Libertarian attitude found in our present-day conception of what media should be. Free and uncensored. Within this New Left there were dozens of smaller movements, one of which is the Pirate Radio Movement.

The Pirate Radio Movement started in the 1960's and continued until the Low Power FM Movement in the mid-1990's. A notable example of this can be found in Brooklyn, New York. Brooklyn saw an explosion of pirated FM bands in the 1970s to the 1990s as the Black Community believed the music and entertainment, they were served by the legal radio stations did not represent their community. This led to countless individuals placing FM transmitters on top of apartment buildings, stores, piles of junk and so many other obscure sites to play music and air opinions that represented the people, their tastes, thoughts and politics.

Similar trends can be found on the West Coast, particularly in California and Colorado. One such station, KBFR out of Colorado, was one of the more well established and organized of the pirate radio stations that led the way in terms of, at the time, a modern and fully outfitted pirate radio station complete with staff, advertising and commercial grade broadcasting equipment.

(KBFR Van, https://apiratemonk.blogspot.com)

KBFR, and stations that broadcasted alongside them, faced renewed persecution from the Federal Communications Commission. In the waning days of the early 1990s, the FCC began raiding stations, jailing its operators, giving them fines and confiscating equipment worth thousands of dollars. This led activists, such as the Prometheus Project, to lobby the FCC and the Federal Government to create a "Community Class" license for those wishing to broadcast on vacant FM frequencies for recreational and non-commercial purposes.

Their efforts, organized under the umbrella term the Low Power FM Movement, were successful. In the year 2000 the FCC made it possible for individuals, small groups and nonprofits to own and operate radio stations. These stations ranged from 1-10 watts of transmission power. Effectively giving a range of 0.5-5 miles of broadcasting coverage. Corporate radio stations saw these new licenses as a threat to their business model and fought hard to stop the program by any means necessary.

While the likes of the Prometheus Project, KBFR and myself would argue that these licenses would help small communities have a platform for free and nonpartisan expression, giving farmers access to accurate weather data (yes I know in the year of our Lord 2025 this may seem corny), allowing free and fair expression of grievances or praises of local, national and international occurrences, as well as giving small artists and musicians a way to share their work with the public, the corporations believed it was the end of their dying empire.

The major broadcasting companies believed that the LPFM licenses would interfere with their broadcast signals. In short, certain poorly made transmitters, untrained board operators, faulty equipment or a combination of all the above, can be a recipe for one radio station's signal to overlap with another's. Basically, if you were to listen to your radio and go out of your favorite stations' range, you would start to hear your station's signal get weaker while another stronger station overpowered it with their content, all without having to change the dial.

While many of the big broadcasters' complaints are pearl clutching, this is the only one I can say has some merit. A lot of pirates and LPFM broadcasters did not have money to properly tune antennas, and at the time had to either build a majority of the equipment themselves, buy them used, or in limited cases from the former Soviet Union. Remember all of this was occurring while AOL (America Online) was still popular, so the Rode Caster Pro was not a standard operating board, and you couldn't buy a transmitter from Amazon. What would cost a few hundred dollars today, cost a few thousand then or a few dozen hours of building from scratch.

Another complaint was that digital radio would not flourish if LPFM continued. This couldn't be farther from the truth as commercial radio stations were beginning to adopt web streaming of their broadcast feeds as early as 2003. Today every commercial radio station has a web feed, and still, no one listens to their garbage! The pros and cons of the debate surrounding LPFM ended falling to the wayside in the early 2000s. Congress after 2007 could not keep momentum going to keep the program in force and in 2013 it lost enough support to where new licenses were not opened to the public [2](Doyle, *H.R.2802 - Local Community Radio Act of 2007*).

The story of media freedom does not die with LPFM; it begins in the early 2010's with online radio streaming.

Online radio really took off around 2007, ironically around the time Congress failed to pass

H.R. 2802 also known as the Local Community Radio Act of 2007. The importance of online radio lies in its accessibility and legality. All someone needed to start an online radio station was $10 dollars to purchase a domain name, have the skills to build a simple webpage with an audio player and a computer. If you didn't have a computer, your local library certainly did. As for legality, the FCC was incredibly lenient with the internet. There was no need to worry about arrest, offending the wrong listener resulting in an anonymous FCC report to investigate your station, fines, or equipment seizures. Where the people lost freedom with terrestrial radio, we gained it and then some with online radio. This would be short lived as a new development to media consumption was occurring around the same time. The first iPhone hit the shelves.

In July 2007 iPhone hit the shelves of American box stores and phone stores, selling over 6 million units in the one year it was available. Other smart phones were sold during the time, such as the BlackBerry and Samsung line of smart phones, however they differed in one key aspect. Apple wanted its users to expand upon the human experience. Apple always had a vision, to break the mold, rebel, resist and be creative with its technology and products. Nothing about Apple was standard, corporate (yet) or normal. The iPhone was no exception.

Music, News, YouTube, even an app for Podcasts was added to the first iPhone. However, at that time the question, "what is a podcast" was asked more times than the app was opened. Podcasts at the time were seen by the general public at the time as fringe, radical, boring, dumb and something for crazy people. Today, it is a multibillion-dollar industry that many people pay me thousands of dollars a month to partake in. This once fringe interest began to grow in 2015 particularly during the gaming channel era of YouTube and the popularization of SoundCloud. The gaming channel was the beginning of a revolution, and many didn't realize it at the time. It was the first time on YouTube that unscripted content became sought after. In the years predating 2015, YouTube was utilized by creators that had productions similar to television and independent films. Scripted, industry standard edited, full cast and crew. Now, all a creator needed was a gaming system, an Elgato game recorder and a decent headset, and they could share their honest and raw reactions while playing their favorite video game. As time went on, this led people who stopped playing video games or wanted to be famous or share their honest moments with the camera to look for a way outside of being a gamer. Podcasts.

As people were setting up cameras and recording awkward and unscripted talk shows in their basements or speaking into an audio recorder and uploading an image over the audio feed to qualify as an .mp4 for YouTube, the Joe Rogan Experience took off in popularity around 2018. Its popularity, controversial content, relaxed nature, and ability to be professionally unprofessional created an explosion of interest into podcasting, particularly during the COVID era when people were locked into their homes with nothing to do. Major Hollywood productions shut down while independent broadcasters powered up their home studios.

Podcasts, especially during the COVID era, allowed for a new level of free thought, experimentation, and entertainment that was desperately needed. With the halting of mainstream media's entertainment channels, many turned to comedy podcasts such as Bill Burr's Monday Morning Podcast, the various True Crime podcasts and other great topical genres of podcasts. When truth became hard to discern, people turned to podcasts such as The Joe Rogan Experience, Info Wars, Secular Talk, The Jimmy Dore Show, Vaush and other relative political commentators of the time. It was through these platforms that average people were able to air their grievances, hear unadulterated truths, lies, opinions, and for the first time in media history the listener was listened too. Shows such as these, and of course with smaller podcasts, valued the feedback and listenership of their audience. The personal nature of independent media has led us to the post-COVID era where Tucker Carlson after being fired from Fox

News, began posting his podcast on X. Donald Trump in 2023 chose not to partake in the GOP Debate for the Presidential nomination in 2023. Instead, he chose to be a guest on Tucker Carlson's show on X at the same time the GOP candidates battled it out on Fox News. The interview between Tucker and Trump had over 200 million views by the end of the night, while Fox News only got 20 million views. That is 20x the number of views attributed to independent media over mainstream media. Similar statistics can be attributed to podcasts of all types, routinely outperforming mainstream media shows during their "prime time" hours.

These podcasts have paved the way for a new change not only in the ways we are entertained and informed, but for a political revolution. In 2015, the early "meme wars" fought on 4chan and iFunny, sites reserved for the most closeted and closest to the political fringes, boiled over into Facebook and Instagram. There were 3 "Great Meme Wars" between the period of 2015-2016. All of them focused on creating the best memes by mocking either the left or the right, sharing political discourse, and refining talking points. These occurrences were initially confined to 4chan and iFunny, being refined and duked out before being shared to Facebook, Instagram and Twitter. One such example of this was Pepe the Frog. Before 2015 this green frog caricature was simply a funny little guy you saw on your screen once in a while. After 2015 he was hijacked by the right wing, using Pepe the Frog in memes depicting outrage, smugness, or mocking of liberals and their talking points. This actually started one of the first meme wars as the left wanted to hold on so desperately to a major piece of social iconography. Routinely the left has failed at maintaining such icons, as well as any foothold in the meme world. Their version of memes are either paragraph long dissertations pasted over a popular meme format or attempting to hijack right wing memes. Their failures are often solidified once these memes are shared to mainstream social platforms and are eventually picked up by the Anti-Defamation League (ADL) and decried as right wing propaganda, "The Anti-Defamation

League (ADL) today identified "Pepe the Frog," a cartoon character used by haters on social media to suggest racist, anti-Semitic or other bigoted notions, as a hate symbol." [3](*ADL* 2016).

(Pepe the Frog, Credit BBC)

The failures of the left to secure control over memes or independent media solidified their loss with the youth and eventually their parents in the 2016 and 2024 election cycles. Often the phrase "the left can't meme" has been used as a talking point to counter liberal attempts to seem funny, slick and relatable. Meme's have been a seriously effective way to convey political opinions, feelings and thoughts to the masses for the last 9 years. To add another layer to this new way of engagement in discourse, people were turning memes and their underlying messages into tangible conversation via YouTube and the early podcasts. This phenomenon, at the time new and scary to legacy media and the political establishment, has once again shown its true power in giving Donald Trump a major victory in the culture and propaganda war against the Democrats, handing him his second electoral victory on November 5th, 2024.

Barron Trump insisted his father partake in as many podcasts as possible with not only Joe Rogan and Tucker, but with Barstool Sports, This Past Weekend with Theo Vaughn, Full Send Podcast with the Nelk Boys, The Dan Bongino Show, Impulsive with Logan Paul, The Shawn Ryan Show, and Adin Ross. Podcasts popular with young men in their teens to mid 30's that created excitement from a frequently disinterested voting bloc. It was in 2016 that this demographic was engaged to vote through memes and in 2024 that this demographic was once again engaged, but through podcasts and their free form, honest and raw dialogue. The Biden Presidency was often characterized by lies, deceit and disappointment. A series of actions mainstream media is well suited for, and independent media is repulsed by.

Podcasters, pirate broadcasters, the FCC and those in the shadowy corners of government know quite well the power of media, especially when it is so decentralized every citizen can engage in discourse. To comment, create, express, and criticize are the cornerstones of any democratic society. Free speech is what gives every American citizen the right to engage in our society and governance. That has been eroded in the post 9/11 years. The FCC cracking down on songs that could be played in the aftermath of the tragedy, the NSA being created to spy on your emails, web searches, browser history, this google drive document that is currently being read by you as a print copy, your credit card purchases. All of these ways to track, monitor, and log your activities. All can be discussed, critiqued, and praised due to the unregulated and libertarian nature of the independent media. Like all movements, revolutions, and ideas, good intentions often get thrown aside for cold, calculated, business and political motives. Podcasts are no exception, although their level of corruption is not to the extent found in major social media providers such as Meta, Google, and ByteDance. Better known by their commercial names; Facebook, Instagram, YouTube and TikTok. Twitter, when it was owned by Jack Dorsey, also falls under this. In its current iteration as X under Elon Musk, it has great potential but still is showing signs of falling victim to the dollar and the dais.

Let's Get Social

Social Media, the blame of all social ills to many is equally the life blood and saving grace to thousands of small businesses and millions of consumers. It is the blame of school shootings and suicides to one person, and to another it is the sole reason they could fundraise money to pay for their child's medical treatments. For all of the negatives social media has exacerbated, it has equally shone light on issues that previously would be confined to small towns and obscure regions of the world. Like Podcasts, Social Media had its predecessor. Web 1.0.

Web 1.0 was the new Wild West. A place for digital pioneers, outcasts, tinkerers, rebels, outlaws and freethinkers to congregate and disseminate their ideas for the first time to a wider audience instantaneously. Typical websites that made up the 1.0 era (1991-2005) were "read only" meaning there was no comment section, no liking or reacting to the written content shared. Accompanying the written content was usually clip art or embedded photographs. Video was not possible as mp4s did not exist yet.

Another type of website in the 1.0 era were chat rooms and forums. Craigslist, 4chan, GameFAQs, IGN Boards, Something Awful and thousands of smaller boards for niche communities and interests were places where people could talk about their interests, current events and share updates from the static read only sites of the time. These forums became incredibly popular, but very few people at the time could see what such a simple, pure and exciting way to interact digitally could become.

The end of the Web 1.0 Era came when the Dot-Com Bubble burst in the year 2000. This occurred because of a few key factors. Firstly, many of these companies were overvalued by investors who were determining their value based off of hype surrounding the web companies and not their financial performance or business model. This led Venture Capitalists to flood the market by investing in multiple web companies that had no clear vision or business plan. This then led to over saturation of the market, where there were more web companies than there were consumers of the web content at the time. A second cause of the bubble bursting was the rise in interest rates from the Federal Reserve in early 2000. This led to major IPOs failing like Pets.com, Webvan, Boo.com and countless others. The result of these companies failing shattered investor confidence, leading to tech stocks on the NASDAQ losing close to 80% of their value by 2002 [1](Hayes & Rasure, 2025). This economic fallout wiped out many smaller web companies as well, forcing the remaining companies to reorganize and retool their mission.

Tim O'Reilly, a pioneer of Web 2.0 in 2005, believed that the internet was a service provider not a place for static pages that mirrored a community board. Tim O'Reilly is a venture capitalist that sought to save the website industry after the dot-com bubble in 2000. Through his media company O'Reilly, he reinvigorated enthusiasm in websites and the internet as a whole by pointing investors to the potential of algorithmic attention rents to generate profit. Due to the advancements in processing technology in 2005, websites had the potential to create more engaging content than in web 1.0. This led to O'Reilly theorizing that addictive, pay to play, content could be promoted to keep users on the websites longer, thus leading to increased sales.

Web 2.0 allowed for third party apps and development to create platforms like Google Maps, YouTube, and Amazon. Interactive applications and purpose for using the web, instead of passive scrolling. This was all possible as new technology like high speed internet, mp4s, Federal programs to invest in high speed internet in the early 2010s and the launch of the iPhone in 2008. Naturally, these occurrences in tech development and sustainable funding in infrastructure, and a healthy dose of skepticism from investors and surviving companies of Web 1.0, allowed for the creation of successful social media companies to take advantage of the power vacuum.

At first, social media was a cool way to combine the beloved forums of Web 1.0 with enhanced technologies that enabled deeper levels of digital interaction as desired from the founders of Web 2.0. This desire soon spread into an unrelenting demand, need and want. This intense and rapid expansion of Social Media's adoption by billions of people across the world has permanently changed society and cultural norms.

The addictive nature of enhanced algorithms has produced a population so connectively dependent that companies both small and large can advertise their products 24/7, affordably and quantifiably. The average American consumes Social Media content over 5 hours per day. Broken down between generations, Generation Z spends over four hours per day on social media [2](Opena & Dudkiewicz, 2025) while Baby Boomers, Gen X and Millennials spend on average 1.5-3 hours per day as a combined group [3](Sheikh, 2025). When looking at this data and keeping in mind the above claims I boldly make, these hours of consumption are interspersed throughout the day. People spend their hours of consumption; at work, at dinner, on lunch breaks, bathroom breaks, car rides, walking, having coffee, and so many other little points throughout the day.

I say all of this to implore and stress that *there is never a bad time to post or run an advertisement campaign.* I frequently see, hear and read "social media experts" claim baselessly and confidently that you need to post or run campaigns at certain days and times. This is categorically false, not only due to the above reality presented by generational social media usage habits, but from an experiment I ran on my corporate account. In the summer of 2024 I conducted a 3 month experiment to disprove this claim. I took all of the AI Generated reels I produced for 5 podcast clients and scheduled them to hit my corporate page at random times throughout the day. I posted 350+ reels per month with no boost budget, no strategy and no care, yet I garnered *90,000+ engagement per month.*

Reach ⓘ   ⬇ Export ▼

120,338 ↑ 10.4K%

(Barone Media Solutions Meta Business Suite April 2024-August 2024)

Top content formats

Published content
Based on up to 200 pieces of content
+820% vs Dec 19, 2025 - Apr 6, 2024
Posts 500

Stories 29

(Barone Media Solutions Meta Business Suite April 2024-August 2024)

This proves that social media advertising is not restricted by time, date or income, it is only limited by the amount you post. The more content posted, the more people will be drawn to your account. This is not to say that dumping content is a preferable strategy, especially in hopes to garner new business, it is saying that the "experts" are wrong and that you as a business owner should not worry about the best time to launch a campaign or schedule a post. You should instead focus on how much you want to spend on hiring a marketing department or an outside agency to produce the content, and how much money you want to put towards Meta Advertising.

While the findings of my experiment seem promising to those on a tight budget, I always recommend clients have a small budget at a minimum of $300 per month to boost posts of interest. This is because the advertising tools provided by Meta allow for greater reach, as well as basic tools to target the post to your ideal audience. Boosting posts or creating a Meta Ad Campaign will take your posts, be they hand picked and finely curated or choosing to dump hundreds of videos per month, and multiply the viewership and engagement by *3-5 times* what their performance would normally be.

Boosting posts allows you to choose the age, gender and location demographics you would like your post targeted too. Meta Ad Campaigns, created through the Business Suite, provide similar tools to Boosting. With two differences. The first is that you can geofence ideal areas. Geofencing is when you choose the township you want to market to and tell the software how many miles from the centerpoint of the town you wish to cover in a circular radius. The second difference is the ability to include dozens of interests your target audience may be interested in. This is a great way to really market to your audience, especially if it is a niche audience. Meta Ad Campaigns are really only applicable to mid to large sized regional and national companies or politicians. The average business owner can see great success with a simple boost of select posts.

One of my clients hires me to post on average about 20 pieces of content per month and provides me with a $300 a month boost budget. With this set of circumstances we get between 30,000-60,000 engagements per month. That is between 35-65% of my experiments results from spamming over 350 posts per month with no budget. Boosting is a far more effective, rational and ironically cost effective way to reach tens of thousands of people than posting for the sake of posting.

This development in the social acceptance of all day media consumption, cost effectiveness of social media marketing and the incredibly low to non-existent barrier of entry, has seriously hampered the growth and effectiveness of legacy media and their sales departments. $2,000 will maybe get you a small billboard or a week's worth of radio advertisements with no way of knowing how many people actually consumed the advertisement, whereas the same money can generate your company 100,000-190,000 engagement and over 1000 website visits.

This is not to say that legacy media and their products should not be considered, after all complete saturation is needed to have a truly effective marketing campaign. Most small to mid-sized businesses cannot afford a diverse marketing strategy, so they rightfully focus on the affordable, yet effective, social media marketing options. The tools provided by these social media companies are life saving and have quantifiably increased lead generation and actualization for countless businesses nationally, as well as personally, with my business. With all of these positives for small to large businesses in the realm of advertising, we must consider the negatives, especially focusing on the consumer of our content and advertising campaigns.

Social Media is designed algorithmically to be addictive. Meta and Google specifically understand that businesses and content creators rely on their companies to advertise their products. This has resulted in Meta earning *$131.95 billion* from companies running advertising campaigns through the Meta Business Suite [4](Rijo, 2025). The needs of advertisers and the money invested by business minded users, absolutely trumps the well being and needs of the average working class American consumer, at least in the minds of the Executives at Meta. In my mind it should be criminal to make such platforms so addictive that the entire fabric of society is shaped simply to sell fucking kitty litter or bedazzled dildos. Humor and rage aside, what are the needs of those who consume the content we create?

As a society we need; community, commonality, and critical thinking. Social Media was initially supposed to enhance the three C's of societal development. Instead, the addictive nature of social media has destroyed these aspects. Starting with Community, the hope was that people could use social media to find local events and cool happenings in the area. While this most certainly does happen, people of all ages but in particular Millenials and Gen Z are at the event on their phones consuming social media content. Beyond advertised events, the same group of people are consuming content while at family dinner, lunch breaks, breakfast, super markets, box stores, and so many more places. Constant consumption of social media has led to these age demographics feeling increasingly that they are lonely and suffer from increased bouts of despair and depression. We are surrounded by people everyday, *yet we feel more isolated with people next to us than alone in our homes.*

We used to have much in common with our neighbors and our countrymen as a whole. Our neighbors in the sense we are at the same level economically, our children go to the same schools, we have the same concerns and hopes for our neighborhoods and frequent the same stores. Nationally, we had commonality as the above was reality in every neighborhood, and we used to adhere to the same outlook: the preservation of social and economic liberty was the patriotic duty of every man, woman and child. This has drastically unravelled with the expansion of digital technology.

Millennials, and by extension Gen Z have been thoroughly influenced by the social programming of Meta and Google. This programming, through an addictive algorithm that feeds you not only what you like, but what Meta and Google believe you should like, has created a generation of anti-social individuals. As a result this generation in particular has abandoned the normal commonality found amongst neighbors and countrymen and instead have placed themselves into decentralized political and social "tribes" scattered across the nation and united by social media platforms.

If we break it down by gender, Gen Z men and Gen Z women are ideologically opposed [5](Blake, 2025). Men of Generation Z are comfortable with the Moderate to Conservative identity with 31% of Men identifying as Conservative and 33% identifying as "Moderates". The Women of Generation Z are heavily Liberal with 39% identifying with the Liberal Ideology and 34% identifying as "Moderates". Specifically focusing on the Men, in the 2024 Presidential Election 16.5% of the independent vote, which in this case I will apply to the Moderates

percentage split,

supported Donald Trump. This places the total Gen Z

Male count for Conservative at 47.5% and the Gen Z

Woman count at 55.5% Liberal. This is in stark

contrast to previous generations who leaned heavily

conservative and moderate across gender lines [6](*A

POLITICAL AND CULTURAL GLIMPSE INTO

AMERICA'S FUTURE* 2024).

FIGURE 3. **Political Ideology, by Generation and Gender**
Percent who identify as:

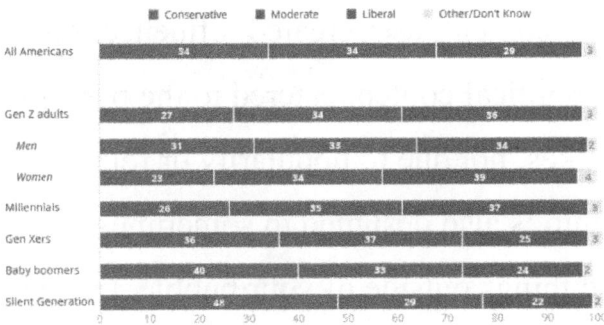

Source: PRRI, American Values Atlas, Mar. 9-Dec. 7, 2023.

This data and the reality it proves is no

accident. The most online generation has been

influenced by an algorithm that promotes two distinct

political echo chambers, so when they come in

contact, disproportionate arguments ensue. This is in part due to the algorithm's construction. Meta and Google created an algorithm based off of the users preferences and likes to better the chances of products hitting their target audiences when using the Meta Business Suite or Google Advertising. It had the unintended effect of also shaping political allegiance and public consciousness. We have such a divide because social media users are addicted to content consumption, an intended effect designed by Meta and Google. This addiction has led to a bombardment of advertised content, user created influencer content and finally political content catered to the persons wants and likes, not due to popularity or relevancy. The algorithm is also designed to sometimes recommend things outside of your bubble, this way new products and services can reach a new audience. This has the unintended effect of different political ideas colliding with an opposing echo chamber, causing increased anger and disbelief.

This has led to a national erosion of commonality. It is why families have been shattered, relationships ended, divorces initiated and mass violence has become a daily reality. We no longer can view each other as simply Americans and neighbors with a shared local and national responsibility to the land, our communities or our people. We have become tribalised, where it seems we live in two nations rather than one. That should be deeply concerning to the reader.

Even more concerning is the decline in critical thinking of the population. The increased popularity in easy to consume, short form media, has drastically reduced the attention span of the average American. In 2004 the American Psychology Association began tracking attention span. When the study was first started, the average attention span of an American adult in 2004 was 2 minutes and 30 seconds. In 2012 they repeated the study and found that the average span dropped to 75 seconds. Within the last few years they found that number again to drop, this time to 40 seconds [7](Mark , *Speaking of Psychology: Why our attention spans are shrinking, with Gloria Mark, PhD* 2023).

With a decrease in attention span, books get traded for 30 second reels condensing a complex issue, movies full of soul and rich in story get watered down to less than 2 hours, and marketing directors constantly battle to make every piece of content memorable and engaging. More importantly, complex ideas are not given the serious thought required to engage with them in good faith. It is why "vanity issues" take precedence over actual policy and governance concerns. A good example of this would be the national obsession over Transgender participation in sports, instead of a litany of other issues such as; an increase in suicides of young men, wage stagnation, collapsing infrastructure, Chinese Communist Party owned Farmland next to US Military Bases, etc.

The former is easier to discuss as it does not require nuance while also exciting and angering both sides of the political arena. It is easier to know nothing and argue trivial social issues than to argue for or against policies that will determine the future of the nation. This is why it is incredibly concerning that the current algorithm used by major social media companies is so addictive. It is harming the fabric of our society and the future of our nation.

As I say with guns, "It's not the tool, it's the man that uses it". Social Media has a lot of good and a lot of bad attached to it. Like anything else, it is a tool that if used by the right person can yield positive and fruitful results. Business owners, politicians, creatives and event organizers can all use social media to positively enhance the lives of those who engage on these platforms. However, the average working person that spends almost a full working day on their phones to consume content is not using it for the best reasons. It is up to all of us, for the security of our republic, the sanctity of our minds, and the future of humanity to have discipline when engaging with such a tool. I have personally removed all social media from my phone and only access it from my computer when I have free time. It has done wonders for my mental health, social skills and productivity.

Dually, it is the duty and responsibility of media companies and those who hire us to create content that is healthy, positive and seeks to break from the norm of what "works for the algorithm". We should focus on content that only does the following; Promotes the companies we work with in a way that matches their culture and products, creates an easy viewing experience for the consumer, and retains our personal creative marks as individuals. It is time to be human and appeal to humans, rather than machines and executives.

The Modern Media Company

In the spirit of Humanity and creative ingenuity, the modern media company takes form. In stark contrast to the media companies of the 20th Century, the media companies of the 21st Century allow businesses and creatives the opportunity to affordably advertise and create. Studio rentals are between $40-$300, compared to the *thousands* of dollars it would cost in the last century. Marketing and promotional videos are an additional service that has dropped considerably low, often the highest rate for a video today being $1500, as opposed to that being the lowest price in the previous century.

These reductions in cost are due to the rapid advancement of computational power and the emergence of digital platforms. Video and Photo were rightfully priced at a premium price in the 20th Century as film development, special effects and long production and turn around times were standard for the media industry. Today, the Videographer and Photographer can charge lower rates as the production process has sped up dramatically. Additionally, cameras, editing software, and computers have become increasingly affordable compared to the cost in the previous century. With $10,000 in the year 2025 you can build a professional and powerful one man media company that can offer dozens of services for multiple high end clients. In 1985, $10,000 would barely cover one or two pieces of equipment for one service only.

(Sony Beta Cam – By KMJ at the German language Wikipedia, CC BY-SA 3.0, https://commons.wikimedia.org/w/index.php?curid=3404297. Valued at $25,000 in 1986)

These advancements in our field have developed rapidly, so much so that people who have experienced our industry predecessors in the 1970's, 80's, and 90's, still believe that the costs for services then must be the same or more today. It is our responsibility as the modern mantle bearers of the industry to properly educate the client on the current economic realities, industry changes, new requirements, as well as current and emerging technologies in the field that may affect their final product or outcomes. Charging prices that are unjustifiable in today's day and hoping the client is unaware of that fact, is unethical and immoral. While most clients today often overestimate the technological capabilities of current tools and expect a steep discount on services, there is still a population that ***underestimate*** the advancement of technology and believe they should pay a 1990's premium on a 2025 efficient service.

Emerging technologies, in this case social media, are often confusing and averse to clients born before the Web 1.0 era. In my work with this population, I have frequently found that their previous experiences with media companies have been abusive and deceptive. Part of their initial skepticism and fear when they initially solicited my services was in part to three major issues. The first and most important issue was the failure of the previous companies to provide an education regarding the products the client was purchasing. This fundamental lack of knowledge, coupled with aggressive sales tactics and promising the world on the part of the media company, led to clients getting scammed out of what they initially agreed too. One of my current clients went through three media companies and lost a total of $20,000 due to the above reality. He was not educated at the time of purchase, was sold a bill of goods that the company could not reasonably provide, all while the previous company hoped he would be none the wiser. As a result this client had his website stolen twice, provided incorrect copies of his brochures and lost thousands of dollars and temporarily lost access to his social media accounts to a digital marketing agency.

Sadly, stories like this client's are quite common among aging small business owners. Barone Media Solutions, as a result, has made it part of our corporate social responsibility policy to ensure the client is educated about the product they are purchasing as well as being transparent regarding the work they are receiving upon purchase.

Part of this transparency and educational policy includes fair and reasonable pricing. Educating clients of the range of cost for services desired is an essential part of the on boarding process. This gives clients knowledge of what to expect not only from my company, but when dealing with companies other than myself. This leaves the client armed with knowledge to protect themselves from companies hoping they are uneducated and can make an exponentially larger profit than the job requires.

There are media companies and public relations firms that specifically deal with Fortune 500 Companies, massive public benefit corporations and other sizable operations. Clients of this caliber require incredible attention to detail, a multitude of man hours, and in some cases a team of people to get the project completed. Additionally, these operations have layers of bureaucrats that have objectives they aim to have realized with the project. Not only at a personal level, but in a way that satisfies the company's corporate social responsibility goals.

This is not to say that small businesses do not require the same dedication and care a major corporate entity also requires from their media partners. Small businesses have less bureaucratic red tape and conflicting personal objectives, making the creative and production process simpler. This is why media companies need to be realistic not only in choosing pricing for their services, but in choosing the level of operations and output they wish to be capable of. Being consistent, firm and fair with prices will earn you the respect of your clients and will lead to more work in the future. Unfortunately, many marketing companies want a "big hit" immediately and will bark up the wrong tree for a $5,000 a month retainer. If your goal is to start a marketing agency that assists local eateries and small businesses, large monthly retainers will not work. Consider per diem or hourly rates for services as these are achievable and less overwhelming for that population. As a fellow small business owner, put yourself in your clients shoes, "How would I feel about paying the price I am charging for the services I am providing?".

If your goal is to build a marketing agency that caters to large corporations, pricing your list of services at a high monthly retainer is reasonable considering the attention to detail needed and red tape involved. Many marketing companies make the mistake of lumping a corporate giant and Joe Blows Pizza into the same category. They are two completely different ends of the spectrum when it comes to needing our services. Companies that understand this will survive and build a legacy for themselves.

After establishing that we as the modern media companies have a duty to educate the client about the services they purchase, the cost they will incur and how it varies across decades and services required. We additionally have a duty to use our decentralized and accessible services to promote liberty and democratic zeal while seeking to expand our companies. This egalitarian goal is not as broad or lofty as the reader may think. There are two characteristics I have in mind when stating this bold claim: helping the client speak their mind and share their vision with the world.

The decentralized and sparsely regulated digital platforms are perfect for a variety of thoughts, ideologies, products and creative works to be shared with the millions of Americans who consume digital media daily. It is our responsibility, once rendered payment, to aid the client in navigating this libertarian and complex digital plain of existence to share their views and have them heard and well received. The attitudes and motivations of pirate radio broadcasters in Chapter One, the aspirations for free expression hoped for during Web 1.0 in Chapter Two, and the demand for fair pricing, client education and corporate ethics in Chapter Three all have led to this all encompassing point: the Modern Media Company must embody the libertarian spirit of our industry forefathers from the past, as we blaze forward into the unchartered, increasingly tyrannical and criminally addictive digital space of the present.

The Future of

Modern Media

The future of the internet, media, technology and society at large hangs in the balance. Since the launch of the first iPhone in 2008 governments, parents, schools, mental health professionals, media companies and so many other groups, quickly realized the major positives and negatives of modern technological developments. These groups and organizations, even when presented evidence of the positives of technological advancements and social media, focused exclusively on the negatives of these new digital tools. As we emerge from the post-COVID era, beginning in 2023, we have seen several state governments enact legislation to protect children from content found on social media and the internet. We have also seen similar efforts made by social media companies, most famously Google in its use of

AI to police and regulate YouTube content recommendations. While on the surface this a good, and long overdue, effort to protect minors from age inappropriate or traumatic content, it may be too reactionary and could lead to suppression of constitutional liberties not only on grounds of the First Amendment, but the Fourth and Fifth Amendment as well.

Google will enact a new policy on August 13th, 2025 that will use Artificial Intelligence to analyze your search history, watch history, and account age to determine what your "actual age" would be. This new approach will override the account age that you declared when first signing up for YouTube. While at first this may seem like a cool new way to solve a complex problem, it is actually detrimental from a creator and consumerist standpoint.

With YouTube's new AI policing system, parents and older siblings will be hesitant to let their kids/siblings use their accounts as they may not get recommended age appropriate YouTube videos for themselves. This means the guardians of these children will have to create an entirely separate account for the child, which may be seen as a turn off to some parents as that gives the child too much control over viewership and could lead to consumption of content the parents will not deem appropriate, that YouTube may deem the opposite. This leads us to a whole new problem: Corporate and Governmental determination of appropriate content.

Current social media algorithms already have the problem of forcing new content in front of consumers. With this new policy, YouTube and its AI will be choosing what is appropriate and family friendly. While current AI does suggest content it thinks you would like, this would be a heavier approach. This is reminiscent of the school board crisis we experienced during COVID when parents across the nation were appalled at what their children were learning in the classroom. This new development in determining age appropriateness on a voluntary platform may give parents an ultimatum. They can either submit to the new changes and even more closely monitor their children's accounts than they already do, or take away the devices and make their kids play outside.

Taking away the iPad, iPhone and Computer from kids is the most logical choice. Especially considering several states have enacted legislation to limit exposure of addictive and potentially harmful content to children from social media platforms. New York State passed the SAFE for Kids Act in June 2024, the bill requires social media companies to use a method to determine a users age based on their content consumption. If a user is determined under age a prompt for a parent to give permission for their child to access addictive feeds is presented [1](New York State Senate, 2023).

Until that point, the feed presented to the child will not be considered "addictive". A similar law in California, Protecting Our Kids from Social Media Addiction Act, was passed and goes into effect January 1, 2027. I firmly believe that parents should take this as a wake up call to start removing smart devices from the access of their children. Firstly, state governments are determining social media to be so harmful they have to make legislation against it, in New York's case multiple laws. New York will also ban Smart Phones from school grounds starting in August 2025 [2](Office of the Governor of New York, 2025).

These laws are incredibly concerning due to the privacy concerns that come with uploading a government ID, elimination of the freedom to choose, and in the case of New York, having to provide justification to use a communication device as per the state education law. All of these infringements on civil liberties by both state governments and corporations because parents failed to be parents. These parents have given the government and media corporations complacent permission to step in and parent an entire generation of children. If you do not like these infringements, do not give your child a smart phone. The incessant need of today's parents to have constant contact with their children or to have them feel included, by having technology, has destroyed a generation and spurred governmental intervention that further encroaches upon the liberties bestowed upon this nation by God.

The request of social media companies of their users to upload a government ID is a major privacy and security concern. The first major concern is cyber attacks against social media company databases. As technology advances in the age of asymmetric warfare, cyber attacks have become increasingly more common. While some cyber attacks target the digital infrastructure of governments and major corporations to steal intellectual property or technology, there are many attacks that occur to steal user data. Your user data, essentially your digital "you" is *incredibly* valuable to corporations, scam call centers, and other illicit or vulturous enterprises. Social media companies, while wealthy in capital and manpower, do not have the infrastructure to successfully accommodate the mass influx of *billions* of government IDs being uploaded by users all over the world. This gap in security infrastructure will make the first 3-12 months of the ID requirements, imposed by government or corporate policy, will be like shooting fish in a barrel for hackers motivated by income or ideology.

Additionally, the final vestige of online anonymity will be completely destroyed. Once the pinnacle of the Web 1.0 era, anonymity and privacy, is now on its death knell. By uploading a government ID you confirm that every like, comment, share and upload is 100% made by you. It is already possible for a malicious individual to hack into your social media account or see who owns an account, what device the account is posting from, the internet provider and the address where the router is located. Adding a government ID into the picture will give these malicious individuals more sensitive data that can potentially lead to identity theft. In this scenario, the malicious individual can open credit cards, bank accounts, take out loans, enroll for colleges and even cosign for a mortgage or car purchase. All of this can happen if someone with some technological knowhow does not like; your opinions, your content or a comment you made. All of this can happen due to a major breach that will occur when ID verification is rolled out by the social media companies and mandated by the government.

From a constitutional standpoint, and this applies only to the United States, there is a concern of further erosion to the fourth amendment and fifth amendment of the Bill of Rights in the United States Constitution. When applying the Fourth Amendment to the Digital Era, we get answers that are not as straightforward. The Supreme Court of the United States (SCOTUS) ruled in *Carpenter v. United States* that anyone who uses a cellphone has a reasonable expectation of privacy as they are forced to passively share location data with cellphone companies in order to access the ability to use a cellphone. The Pacific Legal Foundation elaborates on usage of the Fourth Amendment regarding users of cellphones when summarizing Justice Neil Gorsuch's dissent in Carpenter, *"he discussed how the Court might find that a person has a customary or positive property-related or contractual interest in the records kept by a telephone or other business, and therefore they would have standing to challenge the collection of those*

records by the government without a warrant."
[3](Woislaw, 2024)

While no court ruling exists on the claim and opinion I am about to share, I do believe that Carpenter ought to apply to the government or corporate mandate of users having to upload a government ID to use a service that has become so frequented it falls under *common use.* Much like Carpenter regarding cellphone carriers, there is incredible legal precedent to have a similar privacy ruling for social media usage as its use is widespread and deemed an essential service for many businesses and professions. Such a ruling must take into account how the storage of government issued identification by a private or public entity is subjected to constant cyber attacks. Without the proper maintenance of cyber security measures, this constitutes a grave risk of personal information being leaked (personal meaning a government issued SSID number that is private to you and the necessary government agencies) to those who wish to use said information for illicit purposes. That being said, because we will be forced to upload a government ID to access a common use platform that is insecure I believe that policies requiring ID verification violate the Fourth Amendment.

As for the Fifth Amendment, uploading a government ID can constitute a violation based on the potential for users to self-incriminate themselves. Currently, it is difficult to trace the origins of google searches, or searches on social media, as anonymous browsing and lack of identification to make accounts is the status quo. This absolutely vanishes if the use of government ID verification expands beyond age verification on singular platforms. Google or social media searches, posts, comments and videos, that could be considered criminal, by fact or opinion, can therefore be directly attached to the person putting a query into these search engine options as they have uploaded a government ID. While current searches and content can be traced to an individual, it requires deep investigations, warrants and observation of behavior patterns. Under a future where government ID verification becomes the norm, one search, post or comment can flag you immediately. I believe the former option is the best option to catch truly dangerous people. It requires a lot of pattern observation, and more opportunities to see if the person is simply an idiot or a serious danger. Under the former, everyone who searches for something "criminal" may be treated as the worst case scenario. This worst case scenario would be the use of a government ID verification system against the accused to "prove" they are guilty of a crime as the registered account owner. Due to that system being in place, the privilege against self-incrimination will be muddied at best and completely eliminated at worst [4](Fifth Amendment).

Say you make a Facebook post in a world where we need a government ID to access the platform. In this post you say that you dislike government policies and make a reference that a certain politician or group needs to pay a price. While reprehensible, this category of post is not illegal but would raise red flags. Depending on the "truthfulness" of your identity and connecting information registered on your account, finding the individual would be easy or incredibly difficult. With a government ID attached to every account, post, comment and like then it will be easy to identify "problem" individuals. For the government and the authoritarian minded citizen, this is a great victory. For the libertarian minded citizen, this is a grave concern for our civil liberties. We are already seeing an increasingly alarming trend of the government using the justice system to repress, intimidate and issue investigations against political rivals. This will only expand in the coming years and will come down on the average citizen. Under that scenario, any post or account deemed to be "offensive" , "anti-american", "racist", "pro-communist", etc will have their account traced back to the registered users government ID and that individual will be repressed, intimidated and issued investigations against for airing views or truths that may be "offensive" to the ruling party of government at the time. This is one of many situations that absolutely could and will happen if we do not take a stand against the registration of government IDs on social media platforms. Beyond the privacy and legal ramifications of social media's development, we also have the psychological effects to consider when looking into the future.

It is no secret that social media is addictive. It is also well known that social media is an effective advertising and marketing tool for businesses and a great way for people to get information from a variety of sources minute by minute. Social media at the end of the day is a tool, a tool that can be used to help families in need and grow small businesses or a tool to inflict harm on the human psyche. The addictive nature of social media means that users are constantly scrolling through content at all hours of the day, allowing advertisers access to a captive audience. This reality has led to Instagram and TikTok creating the ability to shop for products on their platforms. This has generated $37.2 **billion** in sales on Instagram [5](*Instagram Shopping Statistics* 2025). Similarly, TikTok Shop has generated $33.2 billion in global sales during 2024, with the United States contributing $9 billion [6](*TikTok Shop Statistics* 2025).

Small businesses and large corporations have used social media to promote their products and services, often saving smaller companies from failure or revitalizing legacy brands for the 21st Century. Stanley, the maker of rugged and reliable thermoses was the kingpin of thermos mugs, cups and flasks in the 20th Century. As sales stagnated due to an abundance of competitors and a fading target audience, the brand needed fresh new ideas for a timeless product. At the height of influencer marketing in 2019, Stanley sold 5,000 Stanley Quencher's to online influencer and Buy Guide cofounder Ashlee LeSueur. A firm believer in the product, LeSueur pushed hard to keep the Quencher in Stanley's arsenal, so much so that she took a financial risk and made the large bulk order. Within days Buy Guide's online store sold out after the Quencher went viral on their social media pages. As of 2024, sales of the Quencher contributed to Stanley rising from $70 million in yearly sales to *$750 million* in sales [7](Vega & Shamo, 2023).

These results were not derived from Radio, Television Ads, Mailers, Full Page Ads in the Magazine or a Billboard. It was derived from a small, yet powerful and popular influencer team catering to women, making a bulk order of the mugs and giving them an honest review on their social media platforms. This cost Stanley absolutely nothing, while revitalizing their entire company and generating hundreds of millions of dollars in revenue.

While Podcasting is a separate medium from traditional social media advertising content, social media has contributed greatly to Podcasting becoming an industry valued at almost $40 billion as of 2024. When podcasting emerged in the early 21st Century it was strictly an audio medium. This changed as video editing software, computer processing advanced, equipment pricing dropped and the COVID-19 Pandemic forced people into their homes and onto their screens. These advances and societal changes led to podcasts adopting a video component to their shows. This had amazing results for podcasters. For the first time, shows could cut video footage into short

30 second clips and garner hundreds to thousands of views. This allows a show that would previously be confined to a local audience or podcast connoisseurs to expand its reach to thousands of new people every week. This only advanced in capability as social meda algorithms were tailored to short content that is between 30-90 seconds long and the creation of AI editing tools, which allow for the creation of 30 days of content in under 30 minutes. Advancements in technology, social media's changing purpose, and podcasting as a medium has not only added billions to its total value as an industry, it has generated over $4 billion in advertising sales in 2024. This further shows how social media has not just helped business grow, it has fundamentally changed the economy and added hundreds of billions of dollars combined in advertising, shopping, and creative projects.

This was all made possible by designing social media algorithms to be as addictive as possible to ensure that content was consumed constantly to give advertisers the best chance to get their product consumed. From a business and financial perspective, this was a brilliant move. Before Social Media became excessively addictive by design, streaming and digital video recording services just hit the market. For the first time, Americans could pre-schedule a taping of their favorite shows and fast forward through the commercials on cable news networks. This sent a chill down the spines of the big television executives and corporations when they realized, *"people can just ignore advertisements we charge millions for"*. This new reality, freedom of choice being accessible to the consumer, inevitably made advertisers look for new ways to beat the fast forward button. They eventually realized that by pushing advertisements on social media, website banners, and email marketing, they could recuperate some of the lost screen time from television and film advertising. Social media companies saw this trend and capitalized on this at the turn of the decade by creating the social media algorithms we are accustomed to today. This new algorithm, paired with the sale of personal data to advertising companies and corporations, has inundated consumers with constant and all encompassing advertising. This shift has contributed billions to the economy, and has made social media and streaming the preferred advertising method. A stark contrast from the beginning of the new millennium where it was feared and looked at with skepticism. While these changes in advertising and consumption have been a net positive for businesses both small and large, it has been a detriment to the socialization of society.

Our attention spans have drastically decreased, children and young adults are experiencing suicidal and homicidal tendencies at an exponentially greater rate than any generation has before them, and political divisions have become near unmendable. It is my personal belief that the over consumption of social media content has led to a society that is reactionary and psychologically damaged. Additionally, political and corporate-social indoctrination has been incredibly easy to achieve as most people consume an entire working day's worth of content and messaging. These realities, once seen as silly conspiracies, are making brands, businesses and individuals rethink their social media use and look for alternatives to meet their advertising goals.

This nascent need prompted my company to create ethical advertising packages. These packages severely limit or completely abandon social media promotion. Clients choosing to use ethical advertising will primarily distribute their content on their website and YouTube channel. These pieces of content will be long form videos, high quality photos and low to mid length text pieces. Distribution of the content will take a nod to the Web 1.0 era, email marketing, direct mail, newspaper ads, and billboards will all be utilized to give the client the best chance of local exposure with minimal usage of digital advertising tools. The added benefit of a package like this, especially for a client focused on creating political, social or cultural commentary, is it decreases the likelihood their content will be censored. Almost anyone who has created content, commented or reposted anything critical on politics, social and cultural phenomenon has been in "facebook jail", "shadow banned", or have been outright banned from accessing online platforms. The ethical package eliminates this major headache for a few reasons.

Websites have only been shut down or seized if there have been severe and long standing illicit activity occurring on them. Having controversial opinions will not result in your site being seized or shut down, especially if the hosting service is from a friendly party. Similarly, email marketing offers a great degree in freedom in spreading your message as you are in direct control of dissemination, frequency and target audience. While print advertising agencies may have a political and sociological bias, a good business owner would run print for anyone regardless of messaging. Afterall, money is green. Yet, the potential client interested in ethical advertising must be aware of the potential that a print advertising company may reject them if the content is obscene, indecent or does not align with their values. While this would be rare, it is not impossible.

The abandonment of smart technology and the quiet step back from social media consumption is birthing an emerging social movement. Younger generations are limiting screen time, adopting flip phones and going on "digital cleanses" where they spend time completely off all social media. This adjustment will only grow in the coming decades as government intervention, algorithm restructuring and prioritization of personal wellness will become quantitative and qualitative in results. The direction of the media is still hard to determine as these changes and shake ups post COVID have only begun to rumble. As of now, I can see in 15 years 1 in 4 Americans being offline, only using flip phones and opting to receive news and information through local radio and television programming, podcasts, and national syndicated news outlets. The era of information overload via social media will come to an end purely due to mental fatigue from constant consumption.

In 1925 the first radio broadcast ripped across the nation with an excited frenzy. Free form, unregulated and amateur, it captivated the ears of millions and birthed a lucrative information and entertainment outlet. Regulation, increasing costs and standardization killed radio, paving the way for television to take its place. Suffering the same fate as radio during the Web 1.0 era, television has finally given way in 2024 to podcasting as the contemporary method of entertainment and information consumption. Social media has contributed greatly to the rise of podcasts, especially during the COVID era when video became the standard for all successful podcasts. In 100 years we have come full circle, we have once again entered an age of media libertarianism.

It is up to you, the reader, to learn from the past. The freedom to broadcast, advertise and express thoughts and opinions has been constantly regulated and suppressed by the government and corporations. Regulation is already happening with social media, it will happen to podcasts next. If you want to freely create and enjoy the content found online it is up to you to teach yourself and your children discipline when engaging with these platforms, to not make it an all encompassing part of your life, and to advocate against censorship and regulation. Government regulation of an admittedly harmful pattern of consumption, is not the solution. It is the resolve of the individual that will limit the influence of advertisers on these platforms and give the government less standing to push regulation in the name of health and safety.

"Only a virtuous people are capable of freedom. As nations become corrupt and vicious,

they have more need of masters."

-Benjamin Franklin

Bibliography

Chapter 1:

1. Morgan, E. P. (1991). Retreating Inward. In *The '60s Experience: Hard Lessons about Modern America* (pp. 177–177). essay, Temple University Press.
2. House Energy and Commerce, & Doyle, M. F. [Bill], H.R.2802 - Local Community Radio Act of 2007.
3. (2016, September 27). *ADL*. Retrieved from https://www.adl.org/.

Chapter 2:

1. Hayes, A. (2025, August 10). *Understanding the Dotcom Bubble: Causes, Impact, and Lessons*. Investopedia. https://www.investopedia.com/terms/d/dotcom-bubble.asp

2. Opena, A. (2025, June 3). *65+ Gen Z Social Media Usage Statistics [2025] That Can't Ignore.* Crop Ink. https://cropink.com/gen-z-social-media-usage-statistics

3. Sheikh, M. (2025, February 24). *Social media demographics to inform your 2025 strategy.* Sprout Social. https://sproutsocial.com/insights/new-social-media-demographics/

4. Rijo, L. (2025, July 31). *Meta posts 22% advertising revenue growth to $46.6B.* PPC Land. https://ppc.land/meta-posts-22-advertising-revenue-growth-to-46-6b/

5. Blake, S. (2025, April 22). Gen z's gender political divide 'creating problems' for their dating lives. *Newsweek.*

6. PRRI. (2024). (rep.). *A POLITICAL AND CULTURAL GLIMPSE INTO AMERICA'S FUTURE.* Washington DC, Washington DC.

7. Mark , G. (2023, February). Speaking of Psychology: Why our attention spans are

shrinking, with Gloria Mark, PhD. *American Psychological Association*. other.

Chapter 4:

1. New York State Senate. (2023, October 13). S.7694A -- An act to amend the general business law, in relation to enacting the Stop Addictive Feeds Exploitation (SAFE) for Kids act prohibiting the provision of an addictive feed to a minor (Amendment A).
2. Office of the Governor of New York. (2025, January). Education, Labor and Family Assistance Article VII legislation: New York State FY 2026 Executive Budget [Memorandum]
3. Woislaw, D. (2024, May 8). *Explaining the Fourth Amendment: What counts as persons, houses, papers, and effects?*. Pacific Legal Foundation. https://pacificlegal.org/explaining-the-fourth-

amendment-what-counts-as-persons-houses-papers-and-effects/

4. *Fifth Amendment*. Cornell Law School. (n.d.). https://www.law.cornell.edu/constitution/fifth_amendment

5. *Instagram Shopping Statistics* . Capital One Shopping Research. (2025, June 3). https://capitaloneshopping.com/research/instagram-shopping-statistics/

6. *TikTok Shop Statistics* . Capital One Shopping Research. (2025a, March 1). https://capitaloneshopping.com/research/tiktok-shopping-statistics

7. Vega, N., & Shamo, L. (2023, December 23). *How a 40-ounce cup turned Stanley into a $750 million a year business*. CNBC. https://www.cnbc.com/2023/12/23/how-a-40-ounce-cup-turned-stanley-into-a-750-million-a-year-business.html

www.ingramcontent.com/pod-product-compliance
Lightning Source LLC
Chambersburg PA
CBHW021625270326
41931CB00008B/875